TODAY'S GREAT QUARTERBACKS

AARON RODGERS

By Ryan Nagelhout

Gareth Stevens
Publishing

RIGHT ON!

Please visit our website www.garethstevens.com. For a free color catalog of all our high-quality books, call toll free 1-800-542-2595 or fax 1-877-542-2596.

Library of Congress Cataloging-in-Publication Data

Nagelhout, Ryan.
Aaron Rodgers / by Ryan Nagelhout.
  p. cm. — (Today's great quarterbacks)
Includes index.
ISBN 978-1-4824-0120-2 (pbk.)
ISBN 978-1-4824-0122-6 (6-pack)
ISBN 978-1-4824-0117-2 (library binding)
1. Rodgers, Aaron, — 1983- — Juvenile literature. 2. Football players — United States — Biography — Juvenile literature. 3. Quarterbacks (Football) — United States — Biography — Juvenile literature.I. Nagelhout, Ryan. II. Title.
GV939.R6235 N34 2014
796.332092—dc23

First Edition

Published in 2014 by **Gareth Stevens Publishing**
111 East 14th Street, Suite 349
New York, NY 10003

Copyright © 2014 Gareth Stevens Publishing

Designer: Nicholas Domiano
Editor: Ryan Nagelhout

Photo credits: Cover, p. 1 Michael Zagaris/Getty Images Sport/Getty Images; p. 5 Stephen Dunn/Getty Images Sport/Getty Images; p. 7 Jed Jacobsohn/Getty Images; p. 7 (inset) Stacy Revere/Getty Images Sport/Getty Images; pp. 9, 13 Joe Robbins/Getty Images Sport/Getty Images; p. 11 Otto Greule Jr/Getty Images Sport/Getty Images; p. 15 Chris Trotman/Getty Images Sport/Getty Images; p. 17 Jonathan Daniel/Getty Images Sport/Getty Images; p. 19 Doug Benc/Getty Images Sport/Getty Images; p. 21 Jamie Squire/Getty Images Sport/Getty Images; p. 23 Streeter Lecka/Getty Images Sport/Getty Images; p. 25 Andy Lyons/Getty Images Sport/Getty Images; p. 29 Ezra Shaw/Getty Images Sport/Getty Images; p. 29 Allen Berezovsky/Getty Images Sport/Getty Images.

Printed in the United States of America

CPSIA compliance information: Batch #CW14GS: For further information contact Gareth Stevens, New York, New York at 1-800-542-2595.

CONTENTS

Meet Aaron

Aaron Rodgers is a football superstar!
He's a quarterback in the **National
Football League** (NFL).

Aaron was born on December 2, 1983, in Chico, California. He comes from a football family! His father, Ed, played in **college**. So did his brother!

Jordan Rodgers

High School Star

Aaron played quarterback at Pleasant Valley High School in Chico. He broke many school records while playing there. He also was a pitcher on the baseball team.

In 2002, Aaron went to Butte Community College in Oroville, California. There, the coach of the University of California football team saw him play. He asked Aaron to play for California!

Big Bear

In 2003, Aaron went to the University of California to play football. He played there until 2005. Rodgers won the Insight Bowl with the Cal Bears in 2003. He was ready to play in the NFL!

In 2005, the Green Bay Packers picked Aaron as the 24th overall pick in the NFL **Draft**. Aaron was going pro!

Waiting Game

Aaron was quarterback Brett Favre's **backup** for three seasons. In 2008, he finally got the starting job. The Packers were his team now!

Brett Favre

Aaron Rodgers

Aaron played very well for the Packers. In 2009, he was picked to play in the Pro Bowl.

On February 6, 2011, Aaron won **Super Bowl** 45 with the Packers in Arlington, Texas. They beat the Pittsburgh Steelers, 31-25.

Top of the Pack

Aaron was named Super Bowl 45's

Most Valuable Player (MVP)!

Aaron had a great year in 2011. The **Associated Press** named him the league MVP after the season.

Clubbing for Charity

Aaron does a lot of **charity** work. He golfs in many charity outings. He's a really good golfer!

What's Next?

Aaron Rodgers continues to break records with the Packers. What will he do next?

Timeline

1983   Aaron is born on December 2.

2002   Aaron plays college football at Butte Community College.

2003   Aaron transfers to the University of California.

2005   Green Bay Packers pick Aaron in the NFL Draft.

2008   Aaron becomes starting quarterback.

2009   Aaron makes first Pro Bowl appearance.

2011   Packers win Super Bowl 45. Aaron is named MVP.

Books

Frisch, Aaron. *Aaron Rodgers*. Mankato, MN: Creative Education, 2013.

Hoblin, Paul. *Aaron Rodgers: Super Bowl MVP*. Minneapolis, MN: ABDO Publishing, 2012.

Websites

Aaron Rodgers' Career Stats
nfl.com/player/aaronrodgers/2506363/careerstats
Find out more about Rodgers' career with stats and highlights.

Aaron Rodgers on Twitter
twitter.com/AaronRodgers12
Follow your favorite quarterback's tweets.

Publisher's note to educators and parents: Our editors have carefully reviewed these websites to ensure that they are suitable for students. Many websites change frequently, however, and we cannot guarantee that a site's future contents will continue to meet our high standards of quality and educational value. Be advised that students should be closely supervised whenever they access the Internet.

Glossary

Associated Press: a news group

backup: a player who replaces another when they get hurt

charity: giving aid to people in need

college: a school after high school

draft: a way to pick new football players for the NFL

National Football League: the top football league in the United States

Super Bowl: the championship game in the NFL

Index